*easy*golf

Jeanne,
To my favorite
mom! Enjoy the game!

Meg Kelly

Easy Golf
First Edition 2004

Tait Publishing Company
8 Lakewood Drive, Saratoga Springs, New York 12866

e-mail: megkellylpga@saratogaspagolfacademy.com
Web site: http://www.saratogaspagolfacademy.com

All photographs by http://www.stockstudiosphotography.com
Manufactured in the United States of America.
Editing by Annie Verbicky
Design and Layout by Joe Arcuri
Printed by Impress Printing and Graphics in Albany, NY

Cover photograph was taken by Tom Stock at
Saratoga Spa Golf Course in Saratoga Springs, NY

Library of Congress Cataloguing-in-publication data:
Kelly, Meg
        Easy Golf: An Instructional Guide for Men and Women/
by Meg Kelly;
        p. cm.
        LCCN: 2004094512
    ISBN 0975599909

To my dad, Vincent P. Kelly, without whom I would not be teaching and enjoying the game of golf; to my husband Doug Mills, for his love, laughter and continued support in my many projects; to my daughter Egan Tait Mills, for her ability to get me to forget about work; and to my friend Carol Lane, for her love, friendship and continued help with Egan.

Acknowledgments

Writing this book has been a great and sometimes difficult experience. I could not have completed it without the help and support of many people in my life.

First, thanks to Doug, my husband. Doug, you have listened to my daily musing about golf and the writing of this book. Your belief in and support of me gave me the courage to put my thoughts into print. Thank you. I am blessed to have you as my partner.

Thanks to my dad, Vince, for always seeing the sun through the raindrops. You are truly the optimist. I love you for that.

Thanks to the many people who helped me bring this project to fruition.

Ellen Bongard, Saratoga Springs, New York, for connecting me to her Vero Beach friends.

Nancy Case, Vero Beach, Florida, for connecting me with the Sandridge Golf Club.

Bob Komarinetz, director of golf, and his staff at Sandridge Golf Club in Vero Beach, Florida, for allowing us to do our photo shoot.

Tom Stock, photographer, Saratoga Springs, New York, thank you for your patience and for flying to Vero Beach to do the shoot.

Joe Arcuri, graphic designer, South Glens Falls, New York, for his patience, layout and organization of this book.

Annie Verbicky, Saratoga Springs, for her editing. Your input was invaluable and made *EasyGolf* a better book.

To all my students who have supported and encouraged me through the years, thank you.

Contents

Introduction

Welcome to *EasyGolf*. Whether you are a beginner or an advanced player, you will be guided through the golf swing in understandable terms.

This book focuses on the fundamentals of the golf swing. Many illustrations have been incorporated to ease the understanding of the language. To make this book a positive experience that will be reviewed again and again, many drills are reviewed. This text may be read when your game has a need for improvement. To improve one's ball flight is a goal for many of us. Your ball flight will improve if you master the *EasyGolf* concepts.

I do hope this book stimulates knowledge and conversation about your golf swing that will enable you to achieve your best possible potential. Ask your golf professional questions. Have conversations about your swing to help you better understand the fundamentals.

Enjoy this book and please let me now your reaction at *megkellylpga@saratogaspagolfacademy.com*. Please let your friends know about *EasyGolf*.

Enjoy!

Meg

Please note: This book is written for the right-handed player. Left-handed players should change the terms "left" to "right," and "right" to "left."

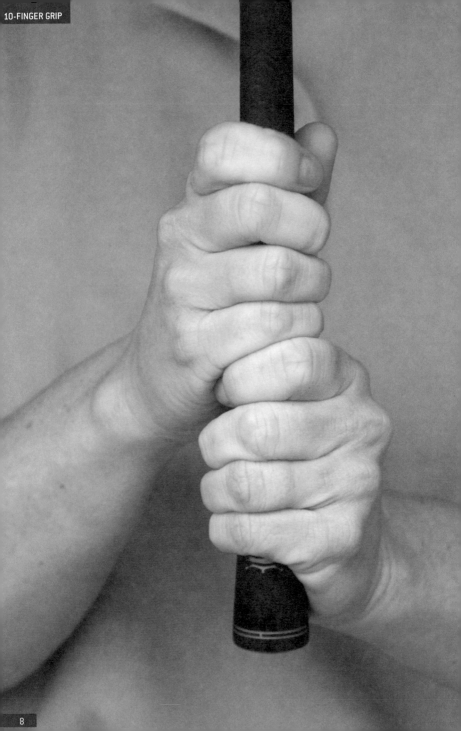

Set-Up

HOW TO HOLD THE GOLF CLUB

How you hold the club in your hands is very important. It has direct influence on your club face position at impact. It is vital that your hands are placed properly on the handle prior to each swing. Both hands work together; your hands should fit snugly and take up as little space as possible on the handle.

The three most common ways to hold the club:

1. 10-Finger Grip: For smaller hands and for physically weaker players.

2. Overlap Grip: For normal to large hands and average players.

3. Interlocking Grip: For small hands, thicker fingers; for the physically stronger player.

HELPFUL HINTS

Hand size and strength vary from player to player. You will need to experiment to see what type of grip you should be using. Help from your golf professional may be necessary. Together you will decide on the grip that is best for you.

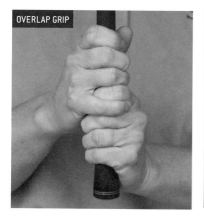

OVERLAP GRIP

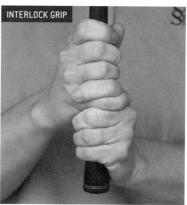

INTERLOCK GRIP

HAND PLACEMENT

Place your left hand at the top of the handle, about one inch below the end of the club. The club lies across the fingers starting at the

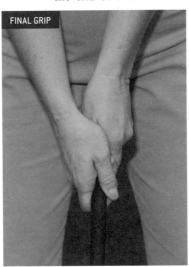

FINAL GRIP

index finger running diagonally under the left heel pad. The left hand grip pressure you feel is in the last three fingers of your left hand.

Your left thumb is slightly down the right side of the handle. The webbed area between your thumb and index finger is called the "V." The "V" of your left hand points to your right shoulder. To verify that your hands are in the proper position, lift your club and release the index finger and thumb. You should have control of the club with the last three fingers.

The lifeline of your right palm covers your left thumb. The club lies along the

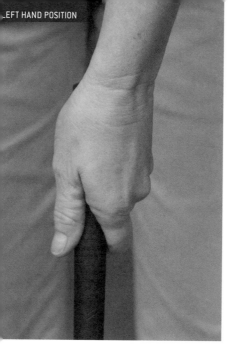

fingers of the right hand between the first and third joints.

Your right thumb lies to the left of center in the handle. The "V" of your right hand points between your chin and right shoulder. The right hand grip pressure you should feel is in the middle finger and ring finger of your right hand.

> **HELPFUL HINTS**
> 1. Make sure that there are no spaces between your fingers.
> 2. Check to see that your right palm covers your left thumb.
> 3. Your hands should work together as one unit as you swing the club.

GRIP PRESSURE

Most amateur players hold the club too tightly, which restricts the hands and forearms from functioning to their fullest. I suggest creating a scale of one to 10, with 1 using the lightest of pressure and 10 using the tightest. Try to make your pressure a four or five. Too *light* a hold will allow your hands to slip on the club handle. Too *tight* a hold will not allow for easy movement in hands and forearms.

STAND TALL

BEND FORWARD

BEND KNEES

FRONT VIEW

POSTURE

The athletic position is the ideal posture position. It will allow you to maintain balance throughout your swing. To create the athletic position, it is helpful to create a routine to follow (see pictures above).

A routine to help you achieve the athletic position:

1. Start by standing tall.
2. Bend forward at the hips. This spine angle should remain constant throughout your swing.
3. Slightly flex your knees.
4. Your body weight should be on the balls of your feet. This helps you stay balanced throughout the swing.
5. Your body weight ratio should be 55 percent on your right foot and 45 percent on your left foot for full swings.
6. Your arms should hang relaxed under your chin.

HELPFUL HINTS

1. Make up a routine to follow each time you address the ball.
2. Check your weight ratio on the balls of your feet by tapping your heels. You should mimic the motion of jumping off a diving board.
3. You should view your set-up in the mirror. Your right shoulder is lower than your left shoulder. There will be slightly more weight favoring the right side due to your right hand being lower on the handle. Your head is slightly behind the ball.

BALL POSITION

You will need to experiment with your ball position to find the proper placement. Everyone swings the golf club differently due to our various shapes, strengths and overall abilities.

GENERAL GUIDELINES

1. Iron numbers 4, 5, 6, 7, 8, and 9, the pitching wedge and the sand wedge centered in your stance.

2. Wood numbers five, seven, nine, and eleven play centered to slightly forward in your stance.

3. A three-wood plays slightly forward of your center.

4. A one-wood plays inside the left instep.

Most amateur players play the ball too far forward in their stance. This will cause your club to ground out prior to striking the ball.

HELPFUL HINTS

1. If the ball is too far forward in your stance, it will most likely go left due to your club face being closed at impact. It may also result in a topped shot running along the ground.

2. If the ball is too far back in your stance, the ball will most likely go right because your club face is open at impact.

3. Look in a mirror to ensure correct ball position.

AIM AND BODY ALIGNMENT

Aim is the common culprit of many bad hits. In the game of golf, you should always be aiming at a target. Many golfers forget about the aiming routine and just strike the ball without thinking about aim.

A sample routine to follow for improved aim (see pictures to right):

1. Approach the ball from at least 10 feet behind while looking down the fairway at your target.

2. Pick out an intermediate target. This should be a spot on the ground 2 to 3 feet from your ball on your intended line of flight.

3. Set your club face square to your intermediate target.

4. Position your body parallel to your ball flight line.

HELPFUL HINTS

1. Only play one shot at a time; think positive thoughts and stay focused on the present shot.

2. Routine is the key to consistency. A solid repeatable routine will help lower your score.

3. When practicing, lay one club down across your toes, step back and make sure you are set up parallel left to your intended ball flight line.

APPROACH FROM BEHIND

PICK A INTERMEDIATE TARGET

SETTING CLUB SQUARE

PARALLEL LINES

Pre-Shot Routine

Your pre-shot routine is comprised of all the steps you take prior to starting your swing. It is important to develop your own pre-shot routine to gain consistency. A solid pre-shot routine will to help lower your score. Once you have a routine developed, you should use it for every shot.

STEPS TO HELP YOU CREATE YOUR PRE-SHOT ROUTINE

1. Stand 10 to 15 feet behind your ball. Look down your intended ball flight line at your target. Visualize your desired ball flight.

2. Pick out an intermediate target 2 to 3 feet from your ball. The intermediate target should align with your far target.

INTERMEDIATE TARGET

ATHLETIC STANCE

3. Take hold of the club, and check your grip.

4. Check your body positions for the athletic stance. Your body should be parallel left to your intermediate target.

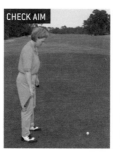
CHECK AIM

5. Check to see that your club face is square to your intermediate target.

6. Take a deep breath, exhale and swing.

HELPFUL HINTS
1. Pre-shot routines are short and precise.
2. It should only take you 20 to 25 seconds to set up and strike the ball.
3. The pre-shot routine is overlooked by many golfers. To lower your score, create yours today; make it a committed prelude to each swing.

The Full Swing

THE ONE-PIECE TAKEAWAY

The first part of the swing is called the takeaway. Your shoulders, arms and club move as one unit. Your upper body will begin to coil; your hips will follow the upper body coil. Your shoulders turn 90 degrees, and your hips turn 40 degrees. You want to feel compact. Taking the club back in one piece will help eliminate excessive movement and decrease the room for error.

HALF-WAY THROUGH THE BACK SWING

This is better known as the "Toe-Up Position." The toe of the club points up to the sky at the half-way point on the back swing. The club should be in front of your right thigh and parallel to your intended ball flight line.

TOE-UP

CLUB IN FRONT

HELPFUL HINTS
1. Shoulders and arms turn in unison at half swing.
2. Stop at the half swing point and check your club head position. The toe of the club points to the sky at this point in the swing.
3. The club stays in front of the right thigh at half swing.

TOP OF THE SWING

As the club continues upward into the swing, your wrists should begin to set into the cocked position. Shoulders are coiled 90 degrees and hips are coiled 40 degrees. You want to feel your lower body resisting your upper body. Both knees should be flexed and both feet stay on the ground at the top of the swing. Your body weight has shifted to the right side. Your left arm is firm, with a slight bend if needed, at the top of the swing. Your upper back is facing the target. The top of the swing occurs when your club shaft is pointing at the target, parallel left of your target line.

HELPFUL HINTS

1. At the top of your swing, your spine angle should be the same as it was at the address position.
2. Keep your right knee flexed at the top of the swing.
3. Your left arm is firm at the top; it may have some flex, if needed.
4. The amount of coiling is directly related to distance.

DOWNSWING

The purpose of the downswing is to release the energy you created by proper coiling on the back swing. The downswing is much faster than the back swing in helping to release your power. The downswing begins as the club nears the top of the swing. Your lower body shifts your weight to the left side from the right. It is a chain reaction. Legs, hips, shoulders, arms and hands build momentum towards the impact position. Arms and hands drop straight down, while keeping a wide arc. You should feel a gradual increase in speed while approaching impact.

DOWNSWING

IMPACT

The impact, position is a more active position than the address position.

At impact transfer 80 percent to 90 percent of your weight to your left side; allow your right heel to come off the ground. Your hands should be slightly ahead of the ball. A flat left wrist is important for solid, accurate shots. Do not bend or cup your wrist. Your head remains behind the ball and your hips turn to an open position.

FOLLOW-THROUGH

As your swing passes impact, you enter the follow-through of the golf swing. Your weight has transferred to your left foot, specifically to your left heel area. Halfway through the follow-through, your hands have released, and your right hand is on top of your left. Your arms are fully extended away from your body. As your weight shifts to your left side, your left leg firms up. Your right foot releases, going up onto to the toe of the right foot, and the toe of the right foot maintains contact with the ground at a 90 degree angle.

CHIP BACKSWING

CHIP FORWARD SWING

SET-UP

24

The Short Game

CHIP SHOT

Developing a good chipping technique is the easiest way to lower your score. I have played with players who strike the ball well, but have trouble scoring. This is usually due to a poor short game. To be a good chipper, you will need to master sound fundamentals.

Set-up for the basic chip shot:
1. Narrow and slightly open your stance (left foot slightly pulled back).
2. Stand with your knees slightly flexed.
3. Place the ball centered or slightly to the right.
4. Place your hands lower on the handle, and ahead of the ball.
5. Your weight should be at 60 percent on your left side.

Your shoulders and arms control the chip shot. Your wrists should remain quiet with very little movement. The chip shot is a shorter stroke, but still requires acceleration through impact.

Your backswing is started with the shoulders; you then return to same position of address at impact. At impact, your weight remains on your left and your hands are in front of the ball. Keeping your hands ahead of the club head will prevent scooping. Do not flip your wrists. Your eyes should stay focused on the back of the ball and remain there, even after striking the ball. There is very little body movement and very little wrist movement in the chip shot.

BACKSWING

FOLLOW-THROUGH

PITCH SHOT

The pitch shot is used when you need more carry time and less roll time. The pitch shot is a low-percentage shot for most players. A good rule to follow is to pitch only when you have to. I feel it is the most underpracticed shot in the game. Fundamentally, the pitch is a mini-version of your full swing. Adjustments need to be made in your set-up to help you control distance.

Set-up for the pitch shot:

1. Position the ball in the center of your stance, or slightly to the right.

2. Slightly narrow your stance.

3. Slightly open your stance; your shoulders should remain square.

4. Place your hands an inch or so further down the grip, or "choke down" on the grip.

FRONT VIEW

The Putting Game

PUTTING

Putting is approximately 40 percent to 45 percent of your total score. Putting is very individualized. Here are some basic guidelines to help you improve your putting stroke.

How to hold the putter:

Your putting grip should be different than your full-swing grip. I suggest starting with a reverse overlap grip.

1. Place your left hand at the top of the grip, approximately 1 inch down on the handle. Your left thumb is down the center or slightly to the left on the handle.

2. Extend your left hand's index finger down the shaft.

3. Place your right hand on the handle and let your left index finger rest on the last three fingers of the right hand.

4. Have your palms face each other.

5. Gauge your grip pressure on a scale from one to 10, with 10 being the firmest grip. Make your grip a four or five.

SET-UP FOR PUTTING

1. Maintain a relaxed and comfortable stance.

2. Keep the ball centered in your stance.

3. Keep your eyes directly over the ball.

4. Hang your arms naturally; slightly bend your elbows.

5. Keep your feet shoulder-width apart; slightly flex your knees.

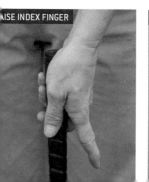

RAISE INDEX FINGER

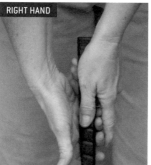

RIGHT HAND

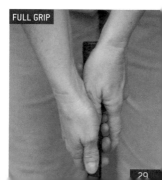

FULL GRIP

SET-UP: FRONT VIEW

SIDE VIEW

PUTTING STROKE

Your arms, shoulders and putter should move away from the ball as a single unit. Keep your wrists firm and the putter low to the ground. Keeping the backswing shorter than the follow-through will help you to accelerate through the stroke. There is no body movement. Look down until you hear your ball drop in the cup. Looking up too early will move your upper body and cause your putter to go off-line.

SET-UP

BACKSWING

FOLLOW-THROUGH

PUTTING ETIQUETTE

1. If your approach shot made a ball mark, repair it.

2. Do not talk while other players are putting.

3. Be ready to putt when it is your turn; line up your putt while others are putting.

4. Stand still while others are putting.

5. Mark your ball when necessary.

6. Step over other players' lines.

7. The golfer who is the farthest away from the cup goes first.

8. Do not use your club to scoop the ball out of the cup.

9. Do not lay your bag on the putting green.

10. The first person to putt usually assumes the responsibility of tending the flag.

11. Lay the flag down away from all play.

12. Give other players space. Stand to the side of the person putting.

READING THE GREENS

Start to read the green as you approach the putting surface. Assess the terrain from the fairway. Look for slopes, and high and low spots. Downhill putts will roll faster and break more. Uphill putts roll slower and break less. Water on the green will slow putts and break less.

When on the putting green, start your routine by looking at your line from behind in a crouched position. You want to view your line as close to ground level as possible. Walk around and view your line from all sides. This will enable you to see the uphill and downhill slopes or the combination of the two.

Factors which will influence the speed of your putt are wind, uphill or downhill grade, and the condition of the green.

HELPFUL HINTS

Wind: A mild wind will most likely not be a problem when putting. You will need to allow more movement on the putt in stronger wind. You need to determine the direction of the wind and strike your putt more softly (gently) or firmly (aggressively), depending on if the wind is with you or against you.

Grade: As I am sure you know, uphill putts require you to hit the ball more firmly, and downhill putts require you to hit the ball more softly or gently. A slow-moving putt will move more than a fast-moving putt. I suggest playing less break on uphill putts and more break on downhill putts.

Condition of the Green: The ball will break faster on a hard, dry surface, so a softer putt will be needed. Water slows the speed of the green, which requires you to hit the putt more firmly.

THE CLUB ENTERS THE SAND BEHIND BALL IN A GREENSIDE BUNKER

OPEN STANCE

BACKSWING

FOLLOW-THROUGH

Playing From the Sand

PLAYING FROM A GREENSIDE BUNKER

The ball does not touch the club in a greenside bunker shot. You hit the sand one to two inches before the ball, depending on the sand consistency. The ball never touches the club face. When struck correctly, the ball will pop out and land softly on the green.

Set-up

1. Maintain an open stance in relation to your target. Aim left of the flagstick.

DIVOT GOES LEFT OF TARGET

2. Place the ball centered to slightly forward.

3. Have 60 percent of your weight on your left foot.

4. Aim your club face slightly to the right of the flag. Open your club face, then grip the club.

The club swings back on the same line as your feet and shoulders. You will feel like you are going to hit the ball to the left side of the target. This swing path feels more steep than your full swing. Once your backswing is completed, swing the club along the same line as your feet, *not* towards the target. Acceleration through impact is very important to completing the stroke. Many players quit on the bunker shot, which causes the ball to stay in the bunker. Your finish should be balanced.

PLAYING FROM A FAIRWAY BUNKER

The farther away you get from the flagstick, the harder the bunker shot will be. The fairway bunker shot is different from the greenside bunker. You will hit "all ball"; try not to hit any sand before hitting the ball.

Set-up

1. Square-up your stance.
2. Choke down slightly on the handle.
3. Position the ball slightly towards the right of center.
4. Put 60 percent of your weight on your left foot.

Focus on the top of the ball. This will help you hit the ball cleanly; do not touch the sand behind the ball. Swing with more upper body movement and less lower body movement. There will be less weight shift. The club head should accelerate through the ball.

Trouble Shots

BALL ABOVE YOUR FEET
Set-up

1. Aim and align your body to the right of the target to adjust for the right-to-left ball flight.

2. Grip lower on the handle.

3. Hold your posture more upright.

4. Take one club-size longer to compensate for holding down on the handle. For example, use a 6-iron instead of a 7-iron.

> **HELPFUL HINTS**
> 1. Make a full swing. Keep your balance.
> 2. Your follow-through should be the same length as your backswing.
> 3. Your hands will be lower than usual because of a flatter swing plane.

BALL BELOW YOUR FEET
Set-up

1. Aim and align your body left of the target to adjust for the left-to-right ball flight.

2. Let your weight rest on your heels.

3. Bend your back slightly.

> **HELPFUL HINTS**
> 1. Make a full swing, keeping your balance.
> 2. The follow-through may be shorter in length due to your bent posture.
> 3. This is one of the game's toughest shots; do not be discouraged. It takes practice to gain confidence.

AIM LEFT OF TARGET

UPHILL LIE

Set-up

1. Position the ball left of your center.
2. Aim and align your body to the right of the target.

HELPFUL HINTS

1. Make a three-quarter swing. Keep your balance.
2. The follow-through may be shorter in length due to the amount of slope.
3. The ball will travel right to left.
4. You will experience limited weight shift due to the slope of the hill.

DOWNHILL LIE

Set-up

1. Tilt your body in the same direction as the slope.
2. Position the ball towards the right of center.
3. Aim and align your body left of the target.

HELPFUL HINTS

1. Make a shorter backswing; keep your balance.
2. Swing with the slope of the hill.
3. The ball will travel left to right.
4. The follow-through may be shorter in length to help you maintain balance.

HILL LIE

AIM RIGHT OF TARGET

NHILL LIE

AIM LEFT OF TARGET

Drills

CHIPPING DRILLS

Nail the Tee Into the Ground

This drill will help you make solid contact with the ball. You must strike the ball with a descending blow, then move your club through the grass.

Set-up

Place a tee in the ground just under the surface, parallel to the ground. Set up in a chip shot position.

Swing

Swing and try to nail the tee into the ground. If you are missing the tee or the tee is popping up, you are lifting the club head too early.

Chip Over Your Golf Bag

This is a drill to help you learn how to accelerate through the swing. Place your golf bag in front of you and chip over it. If you decelerate your swing, your ball will hit the bag or your club will hit the ground before the ball.

CHIP OVER BAG

TRACK DRILL

EXTENDED CLUB DRILL

BACKSWING

FORWARD

Track Drill

This drill is to help you improve your stroke by making solid contact with and hitting your target every time.

Place two clubs on the ground close together, parallel and slightly wider then the head on your 7-iron.

Use a 7-iron or 8-iron. Take the club straight back and accelerate through your shot. Your club should finish low to the ground. The head of the club should follow the intended target line.

Extended Club Drill

This drill will help you steady your wrist through impact. Place a dowel or sawed-off grip at the end of your club, making it longer. Place the extended club under your left arm at address. Using a 7-iron or 8-iron, assume your chip shot position. Strike the ball and do not allow the extended club to hit you in the rib cage area. If the extended club hits you, it is likely that your wrists are too active.

Towel Drill

This drill will help you visualize your landing area and think about how the ball will roll. Many players tend to forget about the roll in the chip shot and overshoot their target.

Place a towel where you want your ball to land. Once you hit the towel a few times, remove the towel and watch your ball roll towards the hole.

PITCH SHOT DRILL
Tee in the Handle

This drill helps you to learn to set the club face earlier. Place a tee in the end of your grip. As you swing back, try to

PITCH SHOT DRILLS

BACKSWING

FORWARD

point the tee towards the ball. This will help set your wrists earlier. After impact, try to point the tee at the ball again.

CLUB HEAD COVER UNDER ARM

This will help you turn and not swing at your arms and hands. Your arms, hands and trunk should move back and through as one unit.

Place a club head cover under your right arm-pit. If the club head falls to the ground, you are swinging all arms and not creating a turn.

BUNKER DRILLS

Aim at a Bucket

The two keys to success in bunker play are:

1. Do not quit at the bottom of the swing or you will remain in the bunker.

2. Aim at something short of the flagstick. If you aim at the flagstick, the ball will roll past it.

Place a bucket or golf towel short of the flagstick and make it your target. This will help you to roll the ball to the cup instead of past it.

PUTTING DRILLS

Umbrella Drill

This drill will help you feel your shoulders, arms, hands and putter working as one unit. It also helps you keep the putter on-line.

Place the umbrella under your arms. Your shoulders, arms and hands will form a triangle. Swing with the umbrella in place. As you stroke to the ball, keep your wrists and elbow angles firm and do not rotate your forearms.

Track Drill

This will help you learn to keep the putter on the correct line to the target. Place two clubs on the ground forming a slightly

wider track than the width of your putter head. Aim the track at the cup. Place a ball in between the track. Make your stroke without the club hitting or coming out of the track.

TRACK DRILL

Putt With Dominant Hand Only

This will help strengthen your left hand and forearm. Increased strength in the left hand will help to control the putter during the stroke. You will see the club head moving towards the target and feel its motion with the back of your left hand.

Using your left hand only, hit three 2-foot putts. You need to be

DOMINANT HAND

focused on accelerating the putter through the ball. Increase the length as you accomplish the shorter putts.

Putt With a Sleeve of Balls

This will help your shoulders, arms, hands and putter work as one unit. This drill moves the club head on a shallow arc, which creates topspin and a more accurate roll to the target.

SLEEVE OF BALLS

BACKSWING

FORWARD SWING

Support a sleeve of balls between your forearms. Make your stroke without the sleeve of balls slipping. Look in a mirror to see your shoulders, arms, hands and club working together as one unit.

QUARTER DRILL

Quarter Drill

This will help you make solid contact. The ball will roll and not skid when a putt is well-struck.

Stack two quarters and place them behind your ball. As you strike the ball, focus on hitting the equator of the ball. Do not hit the quarters.

FULL-SWING DRILLS

Wedge Under Left Heel

This helps maintain balance throughout the full swing. On the backswing, picking up your left heel will create a sway to the right side, which creates a reverse pivot. This drill will make someone who has been swaying feel very confined.

Place a sand or pitching wedge under your left foot. Swing while keeping the wedge in place. If the wedge falls or moves on the backswing, your

SET-UP

WEDGE DRILL   TOP OF SWING

left foot lifts, which will help you sway to the right.

The 1, 2, 3, 4
This drill will help you see and feel the position at the top of the swing. This is a four-step sequence of moves:

1. Extend both arms straight out in front of you.
2. Rest the club on your right shoulder. Relax your arms and shoulders. Maintain your spine angle.
3. Turn your shoulders to the right. Maintain your spine angle.
4. Push the club up. Extend your left arm and bend your right elbow.

Use a mirror to check your position at the top of the swing. Your club should be parallel left of your intended ball flight line.

SWING PATH DRILL
This drill will help you maintain the proper swing path throughout your swing. If your club path is too inside or outside, the flight of your ball will veer off of your intended line of flight.

Have someone assist you while setting up for this drill. Assume your address position. Have the other person lay one club on the ground just inside the toes of your right foot. The club will extend

ONE

TWO

THREE

FOUR

out from the right foot parallel to your ball flight line. Swing back to the toe-up position and stop. Check your club position. It should be slightly in front of the club, but not too far inside or outside of the club on the ground.

SWING PATH DRILL

CLUB BEHIND YOUR SHOULDERS DRILL

This drill will improve your shoulder rotation and help you maintain your spine angle throughout the golf swing.

Rest the club on your shoulders behind your neck. Place the handle end in your left hand. Hold onto the club with both hands. Center the ball in your stance. Tilt forward into your address position. Turn your shoulders back. The handle of the club should pass the ball. Hold this position and check that both of your feet are on the ground. Flex both of your knees and place 85 percent to 90 percent of your weight on your right leg.

SPLIT GRIP DRILL

This drill is for those who slice the ball. The split grip drill will teach you how to rotate your hands and arms on the downswing so the club face is square when you strike the ball.

Using a mid-length iron—a 7-iron or a 6-iron—take your grip with the left hand in its normal position and place the right hand a

few inches apart from your left hand. Make sure your hands are not touching each other. Take a few half-swings while trying to feel and see your hands rotating. On the backswing, the toe of the club should point to the sky. If the toe of the club points to the sky on the follow-through, your right hand crossed over your left hand correctly.

RIGHT FOOT BACK

This drill will help you swing on the inside-to-outside path. This will help you if you swing outside to inside, creating a slice.

Tee your ball up and use a 6-iron or 7-iron. Pull your right foot back about 10 inches. Make a full turn on the backswing and swing into the ball from the inside. Do this a few times; then try to set up in your normal position and swing from the inside.

TEE DRILL

This will help you take the club back on the inside path and swing through to the outside path. It will help you to extend your arms through impact.

Place one tee approximately 10 to 12 inches directly behind your ball. Place the other tee about 1 to 2 inches in front of your ball and on the outer edge of the ball towards the right side. The object of this drill is to drag your club back while not hitting the tee behind the ball. Swing through—not hitting the tee behind the ball—then swing out hitting the ball and the other tee.

HOW HIGH TO TEE THE BALL DRILL

Your woods should be teed with half of the ball above and below the top of your club head.

As a guide, your irons are teed lower; most of the ball should cover the club face.

FINISH DRILL

This drill will improve your balance and give you checkpoints for a complete finish.

Place a book or piece of paper between your thighs. You should be able to hold through the finish without it falling to the ground.

Checkpoints for a complete finish:

1. Shift your weight to the left side.
2. Your right foot will come off the ground. You should see the spikes on your right foot.
3. Keep your knees together and level.
4. Face your hips and knees toward the target.
5. Finish with your arms and hands high.

TEE POSITION

FINISH DRILL

WOOD TEED UP

IRON TEED UP

Setting Goals

It is important to set goals to maintain motivation, to stimulate your interest and to help you gauge improvement.

Goal setting begins with assessment of the strengths and weaknesses in your golf game. Once you have determined your strengths and weaknesses, make a list of three long-term goals. Examples of long-term goals are, "I want to hit farther" or "I want to improve my putting."

Once you have determined your long-term goals, you need to get very specific about how you will accomplish them. Your long-term goals are achieved by creating measurable short-term goals and practice routines.

Example of a Measurable Short-Term Goal

Long-term goal: "I want to improve my putting."

Measurable short-term goal:

• **Practice session week 1**: Hit five out of ten putts in from three, five, seven and nine feet.

• **Practice session week 2**: Hit six out of ten putts in from three, five, seven and nine feet.

• **Practice session week 3**: Hit eight out of ten putts in from three, five, seven and nine feet.

It is important to set your goals based upon your level of play and the amount of time you will spend practicing.

Setting deadlines for completion of goals helps you focus and reminds you to practice. These dates need to be flexible and realistic. When practicing your short-term goals, keep your mind focused on the positive desired outcomes.

THE IMPORTANCE OF PRACTICE

Practice will not make you perfect, but practice will help your comfort level, raise your confidence and lower your scores. I suggest practicing differently every time you go to the driving range. This will help you stay focused and not get bored. The more focused you are during your practice, the better you will play. Fun practice sessions will motivate you to practice more. Remember, practice is for those who wish to improve or to maintain their present level of play. Set goals for all your practice sessions.

Establish a purpose for each practice session. The three basic goals of practice are:

1. Warm up before a round of golf. Depending on the amount of time you have, start with a short club, then mid-irons and finish with a few shots with your woods. This session is focused on getting your body and mind to work together, in balance and rhythm.

2. Working on ball flight. This will include set-up, tempo, alignment and timing.

3. Work on fundamentals; do not worry about ball flight. This is where the most work is done. It will take time and patience under the watchful eye of your golf professional.

PRACTICING TIPS

1. Warm up. It is very dangerous to step up and hit balls when your body is cold. That is when many injuries occur. Start with stretches for the rotator cuff (shoulders), hamstrings (thighs) and lower back. Also include wrists and neck stretches.

2. Set your goals for each practice session.

3. Start with a small swing motion using wedges; keep your feet together. The shorter the swing, the less complicated and easier it is to feel your swing. Hit about 15 balls.

4. Change to a 9-iron or an 8-iron. With your feet in a normal address position, start taking full swings. Pick out different targets for each shot. Hit another 15 balls.

5. Change to a longer club (6-iron). Work your way into the full swing. After a few swings, start working on your pre-shot routine. Check your aim by laying down two clubs to indicate your body line and ball flight line. Hit ten balls.

6. Keep changing your target. Remember, you do not hit the same shot twice on the golf course. Start to think about your ball flight; visualize it prior to striking the ball.

5. Change to hitting your woods from a tee. Repeat step four and step five routines with woods. Finish with another ten balls.

KEY THOUGHTS FOR PRACTICE

I. When practicing, make sure you are technically and mechanically correct.

2. Organize your practice routines. Have practice routines written down in a notebook with different types of routines to follow.

3. Practice frequently making your sessions shorter instead of one long session.

4. Practice with someone; competition raises your level of concentration. Have the other person watch you swing. Give him or her specifics on what to look for in your swing. Play games against each other.

5. Mental thoughts about your golf swing are a very important part of your practice routine. These mental thoughts include such areas as reviewing your pre-shot routine, visualizing each hole and shot that you will be playing and, most importantly, thinking positive thoughts about your swing and game. Positive mental thoughts and images, both on and off the golf course, should be incorporated into your daily routine of living.

6. If you are not happy with your ball flight, stop. Seek out help from your golf professional.

UNDERSTANDING BALL FLIGHT

Understanding why the ball flies the way it does will help you make corrections. There are five factors that influence your ball flight:

I. Club head speed. The speed of your club head at impact will determine the distance your shot will travel. Slower club head speed will create shorter-distance shots. Faster club head speed will produce longer shots.

2. Path. Path is the direction your club is traveling when it meets the ball—straight, right or left. Your initial ball flight direction is the direction the club is coming through impact.

3. Sweet spot. The sweet spot is the center of the club face. Contact on the sweet spot creates maximum distance.

4. Club face angle. Club face angle is the direction the club face is at impact. It can be square, to the left (closed) or to the right (open). The position of your club face at impact creates the curve of the ball, and determines the direction in which it will fly.

5. Approach angle. The approach angle is the steepness or flatness of one's golf swing, which influences the ball's spin rate. The distance and trajectory of the ball flight will be affected.

It is important to understand these factors to get to the next level in your golf game. Take the time to talk with your golf professional to get a better understanding of why your ball flies the way it does.

CLUB FITTING

Would you ever consider purchasing an automobile without first test-driving it and making sure it will suit your needs? Would you just walk up and pay for it without knowing how it performs? For most people, the answer to both of these questions is, "no." When considering golf equipment, your approach should be the same. Buying golf equipment is as serious as most other major purchases in your life.

Before buying your golf equipment, you should have general knowledge of what you want. First, ask your golfing friends about where the best golf shop is. Once you have found the golf shop, you need to be custom-fitted prior to purchasing your golf clubs. You need to be prepared to answer some basic questions that the golf professional will probably ask you in order to determine which clubs will work best for your needs:

1. Do you play golf now? This will help the professional know if you have ever held a club or have any knowledge regarding the game of golf. If you are new to the game, the professional will educate you into the golf equipment world.

2. Do you have a handicap? Letting the club fitter know your handicap or average score allows him or her to have an idea of where you are in the development of your game.

3. What type of clubs do you play now? Bring one of your clubs with you to the fitting. The type of clubs you play with now allows the club fitter to evaluate how your handicap may correspond to your type of equipment. It is additional information that allows the fitter to best serve you.

After you have answered these questions, the professional will want to do a club fitting. Club fitting is properly done on a driving range where you can see your ball flight.

Techniques for club fitting may vary from shop to shop, but these basic areas must be addressed:

1. Proper flex. Proper flex refers to the shaft of the club. A club with a shaft that is too stiff results in the ball flying low and to the right. A club with a shaft that is too flexible causes the ball to fly high and to the right. The ball will fly straight and have a good trajectory with a club with the correct flex. Your club head speed will need to be measured to determine the proper flex.

2. Lie angle. The lie angle is the angle between the shaft and sole of the club head. The sole of the club flat at impact indicates a proper lie angle. With a lie angle that is too upright, impact will be towards the heel of the club, this will cause the ball to go left of the target. In a lie angle that is too flat, the impact occurs towards the toe of the club, causing the ball to go the right of target.

3. Proper loft. Proper loft primarily involves the driver and fairway woods. The loft is the angle of the club face that produces trajectory. With too much loft, the ball flies too high. With not enough loft, the ball the ball flies low.

4. Grip size. Grip size is the diameter of the grip. If the grip size is too small or too large, the student or player will have a difficult time holding the club. This results in golf shots that are off the target line.

5. Club length. Club length is measured from the heel to the end of the grip. With a golf club that is too long, the student's posture is erect with a flat swing plane. When using a golf club that is too short, the student's posture leans over too much and has an upright swing plane.

6. Set make-up. Golf clubs are sold in sets. The set should contain a progression from the wedges to the woods without having any gaps. Golf club set make-up should be determined by the professional and the student and should take into account the student's ability, swing speed and budget.

The golf shop's staff of professionals should personally fit you and assist you in making the best choice in equipment. If this isn't the case, then you need to go to a different golf shop. Remember, referral is the best method to finding a qualified club fitter.

SEEKING OUT A GOLF PROFESSIONAL

The best method in today's golf world is referral. Ask your friends for the name of the best golf instructor in the community for your particular needs. Golf instructors build reputations among golfers.

Speak to the instructor. Meet and discuses your needs, if possible. Ask the instructor all the questions on your mind. Make a list of questions prior to the meeting to make optimum usage of time:

1. What will be covered in the lesson?

2. Does he/she like teaching your level of play?

3. What is the cost of the lesson? Are balls and clubs included in the lesson cost, or is there an additional rental or usage fee?

4. What is the time and length of the lesson?

5. Will clubs be supplied if you don't have a set?

6. Will you be taught golf rules and etiquette?

7. Where does the lesson take place?

Hire the instructor and begin setting goals. Determine with the instructor what you want to gain from the lessons. Set goals, and create a plan and practice schedule. Your comfort level is important to your learning process. If you are not comfortable, seek out a new instructor.

Practice diligently. Do your part in making the game of golf work for you; if you are practicing and you feel your game is not improving after three or four lessons, revisit your goals and make a decision about the solution. Take an active role in your golf education. Do not be afraid to hire a new instructor if your first choice does not work out.

I highly recommend an LPGA or PGA professional. He or she is trained in understanding golf swing mechanics and in effectively communicating them to individuals. For more information about golf professionals in your area, log onto *www.lpga.com* or *www.pga.com.*

BEFORE YOU GO TO THE GOLF COURSE

Before you head to the golf course for the first time, a series of golf lessons will help you build confidence and skill. After your golf instruction, a plan for practice and play should be discussed. Your instructor will help you set a practice and play schedule designed for your personal needs.

You may want to join an instructional league or take a playing lesson to get a better feel for the entire game. Practice on the driving range so you will be ready to play on the golf course. I suggest calling a friend and asking him or her to go with you the first time. He or she will be helpful in getting you acquainted with the golf course operations.

Pick a golf course that equals your level of play. This also can be discussed with your golf instructor. There are executive, championship, municipal, public, resort, daily fee, private and semi-private courses. I suggest starting out at an executive golf course. This is a smaller-length golf course. This will help build confidence and may be more fun.

Call the course prior to playing to find out the quiet times of play. Pick a time you wish to play, and then call the course at least a few days in advance to reserve a tee time. This is also a good time to ask about rental sets if you need a set of clubs to play with.

Golf Etiquette

SAFETY OF ALL WHO ARE ON THE GOLF COURSE

Always be aware of your surroundings prior to taking a swing or a practice swing. Make sure no one is behind you when taking a practice swing. Wait for the group in front to get safely out of the way before hitting your golf shot. If your ball is heading towards the group in front of you, you need to loudly say the word "fore." This is the warning in golf that a golf ball is heading towards others.

Do not walk ahead when others in your group are hitting or are on the tee. It can be distracting to them and dangerous to you.

The golf course maintenance department may be working on the golf course. If the maintenance personnel are in your way, wait to hit your ball. Let them see you prior to hitting.

CARE OF THE GOLF COURSE

Golf course care involves leaving the golf course in the same condition as when you started your round.

Replace your divots. If you are playing a course where they provide sand and seed mix, you fill the divot with this mix. This will start new growth in the divot. If you take a practice swing, avoid taking a divot on your practice swing.

If your ball is in a sand bunker, enter the bunker at a low point with a club and rake. After you hit the ball, smooth all areas. Exit the trap the same way you entered, and rake your footprints as you exit.

Repair your ball marks. A ball mark is made when your approach shot strikes the green. The ball makes a small indentation on the putting green. Use a divot tool to fix the indentation. Insert the tool just outside where the turf has been pushed up, then press the turf towards the center of the mark.

Do not slide or drag your feet on the putting green. When setting your golf bag down, make sure it is not on the green or teeing area.

Keep golf carts on the path when available. Keep golf carts off greens and teeing areas. Golf carts should be parked about 30 yards from the green and tee area and in the direction of the next hole. This will save time when the hole is completed.

Many golf courses require golf carts to remain on the paths; the management may ask that you follow the 90-degree rule: Keep the cart on the path until you reach your ball. You then turn the cart 90 degrees onto the course.

CONSIDERATION OF OTHERS

Consideration of others includes moderating or controlling your behavior. Listed below are several courtesies that you should extend to others, and others should extend to you.

Wait until the players ahead of you are far enough before playing. Don't stand too close when a golfer is playing his/her shot. Don't move or talk when a golfer is playing his/her shot.

Do not walk on the line of someone else's putt. Do not disturb other players with your shadow. Replace the pin correctly when leaving the green.

Get ready to hit while others are playing their shots. You should play without delay. Beware of the group in front of you. If you start to lose the pace of play, step aside and let the group behind you play through.

Keep your eye on your playing partner's ball. Mark a landing spot. Assist in recovering lost balls. When searching for a lost ball, take only one or two minutes, not five like the rule book states. The five-minute rule is for competition play. When a hole has been completed, move immediately to the next tee. Write down scores when you get to the next teeing area.

Cellular phones should be turned off or to vibrate when on the golf course. If you need to use your phone, move away from the other players and make the call as short as possible.

KEY POINTS IN LOWERING YOUR SCORE

Keeping a positive mental attitude and having good technical skills is necessary for playing good golf. Key components to lowering your score are as follows:

1. Stay in the present. Do not relive past shots and do not think of the next shot. Focus on the shot you are preparing to hit.

2. Use your pre-shot routine on all shots.

3. Plan every hole, and give yourself realistic goals for each shot.

4. Play the golf course, not your opponent.

5. Play to your strengths; use clubs that work for you.

6. Count your score at the end of the round. This will keep you from the "all I have to do" syndrome.

7. Be patient with yourself. All shots are not great ones. Remember to stay in the present; look at each shot.

HOW TO FIGURE YOUR HANDICAP

First, you need to understand equitable stroke control (ESC).

ESC puts a lid on the number of strokes that you can count on a hole (for handicapping purposes):

Zero to nine handicap: You can take nothing higher than a six on a single hole.

10 to 19 handicap: Seven or under.

20 to 29 handicap: eight or under.

30 to 39 handicap: nine or under.

If the player with a 35 handicap on a par three shoots a 12, he/she may only score a nine.

If the player with a 17 handicap on a par three shoots a nine, he/she may only score a seven.

Remember, this is only for handicapping purposes.

Once you have accurately recorded a score, the next step is to calculate the differential. This is done by subtracting the course rating from your ESC score.

The course rating is what a scratch player would be expected to shoot.

For example:

Course rating: 72.1

My ESC score: 97

Differential: 24.9

24.9 multiplied by 113 (113 is an average for course rating) is 2813.7.

2814 divided by 138 is 20.38.

This is not your handicap. You need to post 20 scores and have 20 differentials. Take the average of your 10 lowest scores. When you have more then 20 rounds, take the lowest 10 scores from the 20 most recent rounds.

This all sounds very complicated; it is. Have someone do it for you. Ask your golf course if it offers the USGA handicap system. You may join the USGA handicap system for a fee at your golf course.

SLOPE RATING

A course's slope rating is based on the number of hazards, fairway length, course topography, prevailing wind, etc. An average course rating is 113. An easy course would be rated around 90. A harder course would be rated up to 150.

If your home course handicap index is 13.6, your handicap might go up to a 16 when playing a 135 slope-rated course.

If you play a course rated 95 slope (an easy course), your handicap will go to a 10. At an easy course, your handicap will likely go down. At a hard course, your handicap will likely go up. On the scorecard, you will see two sets of numbers: for example, 72.1 rated/slope 138. The first number will indicate a scratch player's score. The second number reflects the level of difficulty of the course (slope).

Glossary

Understanding golf terms will help you mingle with other players and "talk the talk" in golf. You will not feel comfortable on the course unless you understand golf's terms and phrases. The following terms will give you a better understand of the game of golf.

BALL FLIGHT TERMS

Draw: A mild right-to-left ball flight.

Fade: A mild left-to-right ball flight.

Fat shot: Hitting the ground before the ball, causing the ball to travel a shorter distance. Also called a "chili dip" or "chunk shot."

Hook: A shot curving severely right-to-left.

Push: A shot that goes right of the target with no curve.

Pull: A shot that goes left of the target with no curve.

Shank: A shot hit on the neck or hosel of the club, causing the ball to go severely to the right (and usually low).

Slice: A shot curving severely left-to-right.

Thin shot: Hitting high on the ball, causing the ball to go low and run along the ground; also called a "skulled shot," "bladed shot" or "topped shot."

Yips: A condition in putting in which the player is fearful of the results. A jerky stroke is made.

SCORING TERMS

Ace: Holing out after one shot; also called "hole in one."

Albatross: A score of three under par; also called a double eagle.

Birdie: Scoring one shot less than par on an individual hole.

Bogey: Scoring one shot over par on an individual hole.

Dormie: A term used in match play for the situation in which a player or team is leading by as many holes as there are left to play, and therefore cannot be beaten.

Double eagle: A hole score of three strokes less than par.

Eagle: A score of two less than par on a hole.

Gimme: A putt short of the hole that is conceded by a golfer's partners. Gimmes do not exist under the rules of golf.

Greenies: A betting game awarded on par threes to the player closest to the hole on his or her tee shot.

Gross score: The actual number of shots on a hole or round before handicap is subtracted.

Handicap: The number of strokes a golfer receives to equalize competition between a poor player and a better player.

Hole in one: A tee shot that finishes in the hole.

Medalist: The lowest individual score in a stroke play tournament.

Mulligan: Playing a second ball from the same spot as the first. Mulligans do not exist under the rules of golf.

Net score: Your gross score minus your handicap.

Par: A score a good player would be expected to make on a hole.

Penalty strokes: Strokes added to your score as a result of a rules violation.

Quadruple bogey: A hole score of four over par.

Sandbagging: Playing poorly on purpose to get a higher handicap.

Scratch player: A player with great skill and a zero handicap.

Skins: A betting game in which the amount of money is won by the player with the lowest score on a hole.

Triple bogey: A hole score of three strokes over par.

Whiff: To swing and miss the ball completely. This counts as a stroke.

GOLF COURSE TERMS

Apron: Short-cut grass encircling the putting green. Also called the "collar" or "fringe."

Back nine: The second nine holes in an 18-hole round.

Bunker: A depression in the fairway, rough or the green. It can be filled with grass or sand.

Divot: A piece of grass removed from the ground by the club head at impact.

Fairway: The short-grass area that is the intended route from tee to green.

Flagstick: The pole and flag placed in the hole's location on the green.

Fringe: The short-cut grass encircling the putting green; also called the "collar" or "apron."

Front nine: The first nine holes in an 18-hole round.

Grain: The direction of the grass on the putting green lies.

Green: A short, grassy area used for putting that is located at the end of each hole.

Green keeper: The superintendent of the grounds crew; also called the golf course superintendent.

Hazard: The sandy or watery areas on the golf course.

Hole: A round opening on the putting green that is 4 ¼ inches in diameter and 4 inches deep.

Lip: The edge of a bunker or of a hole.

Rough: The tall grass that borders the fairway and surrounds the green.

Teeing ground: The area of short grass from which play begins on a hole.

NOTES

NOTES

NOTES